LISA ANNABEL

and i felt it all

outskirts
press

Prologue

To feel it all is to sit with yourself and allow all the unresolved grief pour out from your soul. Grief that you didn't realize was dormant and waiting to be healed. It means to try to allow yourself to be open to the possibilities that come after love. I don't mean another person, I mean the possibilities of reinventing yourself. Of growing. Of letting go of who you were and becoming a more healed version of yourself.

What I have learned from my grief is that I am no longer the person I once was before the heartache. A part of me dies with the deep love I have for someone when they are gone.

This is my healing story through poetry and essays. My writing helped me discover a version of myself that I didn't know could exist. That I didn't know needed help unraveling the grief that was tangled within me.

Feeling all of my emotions has taught me to live for myself in a way that I can gently walk through this world.

We are faced with many challenges, and those challenges will bring heartache. Through these challenges our heart will require us to lean inward and repair our wounds. How we repair, how we heal, will be reflected in how we interact with the world afterward.

Healing is not beautiful. Healing is messy. It is the tears that no one sees. It is the intrusive thoughts you would rather keep to yourself. To heal is to address the pain we feel within and at times may seem so slow. To heal is to focus our pain and turn it into love. A love we can have for ourselves.

Nothing prepared me for the deep loss that would have his name, but it has given me an opportunity to discover a deeper connection with the broken-hearted. A connection that has taught me a love for myself I didn't know I needed.

love

loss

lessons

How did they get here?
What does she call him now?
He was all that she needed and all that she
knew how to be.
Instead of sending a search party for them,
they gave in and let the tidal waves take them
under.
They were never to be seen again. In the
undertow, the current beneath the surface
forced them to be a new version of themselves.
Versions they didn't think they would ever
meet.
Fortunately or unfortunately, their story didn't
have a soft ending. She takes time to accept this
hard truth.
She gave up on many things to learn how to
love him. In the middle of their relationship,
she gave up many parts of herself to be loved
by him.
The process of change forced her to turn
inward and accept that she didn't know how to
love herself, so how could she have expected
that from him.
When the relationship felt uncomfortable, she
would quiet the voice within her asking her
to set a boundary. The lines became blurred,
and she internalized that, in order to be loved,

she needed to keep others happy before her genuine joy. As the years passed, she put his comfort before her own. Unknowingly, she nurtured unhealthy patterns to keep from destroying the potential of their future together…a future that she built alone.

Making herself small wouldn't save her from the lonely ocean she was in.
She was going to lose him all while losing herself too.
She realized many truths in the process of accepting and letting go.
Truths that skewed her religious views.
Love shouldn't endure all things. If it does, then is it really love? Enduring means to patiently suffer. She did just that and paid a high price to build a new stable relationship for herself.
Love shouldn't bear all things. Accepting something that is unpleasant isn't love.
She accepted a relationship that left her with both good and bad. The bad gave her the lessons she now carries moving forward.
Love shouldn't believe all things. Believing all things is to not see the reality that was laid out before her without question.
How she wishes she knew these lessons before

giving all of herself just to keep him.
She was scared to be here.
Alone.
Starting over not knowing what to call him.
It was inevitable to end up here, trapped in her
emotions between what she thought was love
and now knows as pain.

it was then that i understood,
a change was happening in july.

with tears in our eyes and a storm within my
soul, i couldn't help but say goodbye.

contemplating…

should i hold on and stay?
or abandon and walk away?

deciding for me is not beautiful
this feeling is immutable

choosing me is so hard
and it comes with no regard.

this time i will put myself first,
even when it hurts.

(july thoughts)

i can't fulfill your needs
and so,
insecurity breeds
i can't control my mind
in a constant place
that's misaligned
we both grew weak
unable to speak
you and i
slowly grew apart
and that's what broke my heart

(jealousy)

running back to what's familiar
settling
difficult to reconfigure
this is threatening

hopeless
the lack of interest
leaves me restless

i hold on to new people
directionless
it almost feels lethal

the dead end is clear
i fear the not having someone near

i beg them to stay
the price for this attachment i will pay

(toxic bond)

And I Felt It All

a million miles away
yet you are near

what happened?
the picture isn't clear

the air feels heavy
it's hard to breathe
i want you here
but we lost the intimacy

the seasons changed
yet the bloom of spring i felt for you didn't
return
a distance lives deep within me

is it time to let go?

(distance between)

there's a whisper in the roses...
telling the most delicate lies
blindly charming, she is not yet wise
blooming only harm
instinct sounding the alarm

roses...
slowly wilting
leaving only thorns
her heart mourns
suffering with all her fears
softly wiping her tears as their end nears

there's a whisper in the roses...
she can now hear
your end isn't here, my dear

(broken rose-colored glasses)

cobalt blue
that was my love for you
rare.
little did i know
it would cease to grow
just like the wilted rose that sits lonely in a
vase
i sit with despair.
she lets me wallow in my sorrow
with my heart in my hands
hollow

(oxidized love)

broken
but still open

maybe this time i stay
and risk the fall
…
unspoken
but i keep hoping

maybe this time i stall
to avoid the fall

torn
all because of you

(blame)

moving through emotions

"We run to undo the damage we've done to body and spirit. We run to find some part of ourselves yet undiscovered." -John Bingham

She is a runner. She runs for no one, but herself. She runs because right now, it is the only thing she can control in the midst of her life spiraling out of control.

As she laces up her shoes, she can't help but go deep within her mind where all her questions, fears, and insecurities linger. She tries to process all of the heaviness of her emotions she carries after a breakup. Her eyes begin to water as she takes a deep breath and gently exhales into the reality of her life alone.

She presses play on her favorite playlist in hopes of getting through her run. In hopes of taking her mind off the questions that were left unanswered. She wipes her tears and embraces the freedom of her feet hitting the pavement. She promised herself that this time she wouldn't stop no matter the pace. After all, she knows that life continues with or without her being fully present. She hopes that with this commitment to herself, she can gradually grow with every run.

No obstacle will hold her back from giving herself the joy that walked out the door with him. She will not give up on herself. She longs to love herself, and this run was going to be proof of that self-love. He may not have loved her as she deserved, but she'll be damned if she doesn't pick herself up and move forward with her life. Funny how after a breakup she can't help but notice the faults and failures that could have been changed.

She is learning that it is up to her to learn how to love the best and worst parts of herself. She is learning that life is not about striving to be perfect. Maybe it's about loving the imperfect person that she sees in the mirror. Maybe love toward herself is the one love nobody can take from her.

In the middle of her heartache, she discovered running so she can discover the love she deserves to have for herself.

And I Felt It All

i sit and stare.
my life in review
and all i see is you.

like a wave crashing
our time spent together was stopping.

i don't know what to do.
so i go out.
i catch a breath of fresh air.

knowing what i know,
i ask myself, is there room to grow.
deep in my heart the answer is no.

i sit and stare.
this is what it feels like
in the hour of despair.

(in the hour)

i didn't want anyone else
i didn't need to try others
because he knew
how to fit

like the last puzzle piece that completed my life

i didn't want anyone else
i bent my boundaries to keep him
because to me
he was my everything

but

like the sunset ending daylight

i didn't want to be me anymore
i lost the most important pieces of me

so i began to search
for pieces of peace

(lost & found)

eyes filled with tears.
a heart full of pain.

goodbyes are so difficult to navigate.

i don't know what i'm doing wrong.
or maybe i do.

i try to fix the broken.
the broken that doesn't want to be fixed.
sometimes the pain of loneliness is heavier
than the need to walk away.

but i'm learning,
so i leave you here.

i can't enter a home that's filled with fears.
fears that only cause me tears.

(patterns of wrong love)

So, what is love?

Love is seeing reality and trusting in ourselves.
Love is listening when we need to take a step
back and protect ourselves from harm.
Love is knowing that we will only believe truth
through aligned words and actions.
Love is accepting our realities and moving
through life accordingly.

Lessons of love are all that remains.
Regardless of how they ended, they are both
worthy of love from another, but mostly a
better love for themselves.
Although the chapter they shared was brief,
their story will forever be bittersweet.
Maybe she will never know what to call him…
and maybe that's another thing she must
accept.
Acknowledging this truth brings her tears of
strength.
Strength to know that she can overcome
challenges with grace.

making meaning

She invites curiosity from others as an opportunity to further heal her wounds. As she sits across the table from another woman who seeks to understand why she didn't "fight" for her relationship, she realizes that there will be aspects of our lives that nobody will understand other than those who lived it together.

Even then, each person in the relationship holds their own version of how it all happened.

As the two women engage in conversation about love, the woman's curiosity brings simple, yet complicated questions. Questions that she has to sit with for a while to fully respond.

Why did it end?

It was time. I finally acknowledged the side
in him that I tried hard not to see. As well as a
side within me. It was as if I blinded myself to
avoid saying that it wasn't the right fit for me.
That acknowledgment was the most painful
realization in my adult life.
Putting my own needs aside in order to keep
the peace was suffocating me every day.
It is a pain that unveils who we had become
and who I no longer wished to be.

Did you stay in touch?

The short answer, no.
The complexity that lies within me…I loved so deeply that all I could do was let go so I could grow.
In a society that is closely tied together through technology, attachment is so easy. The ability to stay connected can be detrimental to our progress of self-discovery.
Sometimes the best thing we can do with somebody we loved so deeply is to truly let go. To forgive ourselves for the hurt we caused and make peace with what didn't work out.
All of which leads to acceptance.
I think the fear of moving into the unknown tends to make us hold on to our past. We hold on to previous lovers, spouses, etc. so we feel less alone.
I am here to tell you that it's okay to be alone and allow yourself to rediscover a person you left behind.
I wish him nothing but goodness and progress.
I am okay without seeing that firsthand.
After all, letting go is love.

Did you find closure or does it still hurt?

Years later that included pain and many changes, that question still catches me off guard. However, it is easier to hold back the tears now. I think we slowly develop coping mechanisms to be able to move forward.
My coping mechanism for these moments is reminding myself of what I have done with the time passed. I discovered a version of myself that lives life for herself. That gives to others wholeheartedly and goes after her goals. I don't know how long the pain will stay, but I know that with time it will slowly fade away.

So did I find closure?

I take a deep breath and respond with a
question: do we find closure, or do we decide
to make closure?
In this case, I made my own closure.
Closure to the loneliness I felt because I lost the
most important person in my life. Me.
Closure to the illusion of the future I thought I
wanted, but accepted that it wasn't a reality.
Closure to my past, so I could build a brighter
future to be free.

Experiencing pain opens the door to healing and growth. I take pride in this humbling experience. It takes courage to let go, heal for yourself, so that in return you can learn to love.
A love that is reflected in all of your relationships both past and present.

loyalty is letting go.
like a rose in a vase wilting with time.
it's releasing a love that is no longer mine.

loyalty is learning how to flow
like the crash of a wave that clears the shore.
it's gripping a love that gives no more.

loyalty is letting go of you to find me.
because i know it's no longer we.

(loyalty is freedom)

"Grief does not change you, […]. It reveals you."
– John Green

They tell her that what she is going through are
the stages of grief. She hasn't brought herself
to actually look up the stages. Knowing them
won't change her pain.

She has felt grief. She knows that pain all too
well. She knows that loss of a loved one is
painful, and there will always be a void in her
heart for their absence.
But this.
This does not feel anywhere near grief.
This pain has only his name.

What she feels right now causes her to
entangle her mind with insecurities, doubts,
and sadness. It is a debilitating pain that can
only find relief by ripping her heart out, gently
setting it on a table to rest, to help her catch her
breath. Even if it is just for a moment.

She is learning that a divorce is grieving
multiple aspects of your life, and nobody asked
if you were ready to endure the pain.
You grieve your plans that have become
nonexistent.
You grieve your home.
You grieve your life as a wife.
You grieve a living person who you know isn't
good for you...
You grieve the you who left with them.

However, she had to love herself because he
didn't know how to love her. She understands
that others can only love to the capacity they
love themselves. To her misfortune, his lack of
love causes her to feel a pain that isn't grief.
She searches for a word to name the pain she
feels every day. For now, it carries his name.

Nevertheless, in the middle of this pain, she
finds another fragment of her shattered soul,
and she softly puts it in its place.
That's when she realizes that she can harness
this pain to grow.

She wipes her tears.

Takes a deep breath.

Lifts herself up and reminds herself that this too shall pass.

And when she meets herself on the other side, she will know it was all a part of the process to be set free.

reflection & healing

"My family is not running a marathon. We're running a relay. My parents have gotten me this far. Everything I do is to get us further. I carry their hopes along with my own."
—Maria E Andreu

As the youngest of four girls, she knew she was different. Emotionally she felt like a foreigner in her own home. A foreigner who dreamt of having a different life. A life where she could express her emotions and not be sent to her room until the tears were dry. A life where she could be understood and not judged for her mistakes. Her parents raised them with cultural expectations from their country, not hers. Thinking back she sees it as a gift because she is able to connect to an extended family that lived in a different country hundreds of miles away. She knows her parents did their best. They provided more than they ever thought they could provide. She understands the love they gave was through hard work and tough love. A tough love that was rooted in broken homes where there were cycles of generational trauma.

Cycles she recognized that didn't need to be repeated.

Her father was raised by a single mother,
which forced him to grow up too quickly.
Working to provide for his siblings and mother
by the age of twelve.
Her mother lost both of her parents before the
age of sixteen and was raised by her sisters,
who also grew up too quickly.
Her parents carried these traumatic
experiences with them into their marriage.
Her first model of love. A love that reflected
suppressed emotions, unhealed wounds, and
resentment.
If she could only give her parents the
childhood they deserved. The security
that's built through unconditional love. The
nurturing of a mother and father.
The only thing her parents wanted was to raise
their daughters to be better than themselves.
However, it was the conditioning of being a
"good girl" that created a lack of self-love.
A conditioning that means to hide your own
needs to please others. To be…quiet, obedient,
free from failures.
Her parents unknowingly placed expectations
that led to her struggle with perfectionism.
Perfectionism that led to people-pleasing and a
false sense of security.

She wanted a marriage that was not like her
parents. She wanted to share open, calm
communication and an authentic connection.
A healthy marriage that worked through the
struggle.
A marriage that was not familiar to her.
Her divorce broke the idea of perfection and
opened unhealed familial wounds she didn't
even know existed. She knew she would have
to run toward her storm and that it would
require her to let her family down in order to
build a healed version of herself. A version
that would heal unhealthy generational cycles.
Cycles that were the opposite of being quiet
or obedient. She would need to face failures
without fear.
This is first generation trauma in regard to
love.

coffee — black
rattle of a spoon among the stillness.
4 a.m. conversation about life and her illness.

rough hands with mine.
smell of a summer storm.
silently thinking that life without her will
transform.

a raspy voice won't be echoed again.
left with only memories of then.

love that taught me grief.
pain that feels like it has no relief.

(my first loss)

you held me close
yet, intimately we were so far away
adult and child
a bittersweet bond we would later pay
child and adult
i didn't know i would spend a lifetime looking
for your love in my mates
yet, i wasn't okay with that fate
past and future
i lived my life to obey
little did i know it was the me i would betray
future and past
gracefully, i began to let go of the fear of your
rejection
so i embraced my imperfections
dependent to free
i began to show you the real me
as we move forward in this phase i know we
will be
mother and daughter
that's the you i love in me

(my wound)

i cried and you held me
the best way you knew how

not gently
a hold tight enough to know i wasn't alone

you told me to wipe my eyes
look up
reminded me to love me

you didn't promise me roses
you showed me strength

passed no judgment
you knew how i was breaking

showed me unconditional love

(love)

lost without a road map
a heart filled with guilt.

all i want to do is cry in your lap,
tell you that the life i built
wasn't for me, but for you.

have i failed you because this time i will choose
me?
the heaviness i feel makes me question...
Will these choices set me free?

(children of immigrants)

torn between two worlds.
mine and yours.

this place wasn't set for me to win.
i hold space for this pause.

i let go of expectations.

that's the difference between your world and
mine.
i don't believe in them.
they no longer fit with me.

you taught me to be brave.

i no longer seek your permission to find the me
that lives within.
discover what is important to me.
recognize what i am okay with and what just
doesn't sit with me.

i wasn't taught to turn inward,
yet i am brave enough to pull myself through.

my worth isn't defined by my elders
or you...

my growth hurts
it's uncomfortable

i hold space for this pause
i deserve it.
i know i seem lost.

Trust me when i say,
it is painfully beautiful to be me.

(breaking open)

"Rivers know this: there is no hurry. We shall get there some day."
— A.A. Milne

Time stood still. She knew it was time to end what was breaking her for some time. She silently packed her attachments to a future that she had patiently waited for and never came. She walked out on the relationship that no longer existed.

It hurt her then and still does now. Sometimes. The memory of them comes to mind in waves, but with less tears.

In the end, there was no argument. There was simply a heavy silence. He knew that she was a once in a lifetime, so he asked to be friends. However, she loved him so much that she couldn't be his friend. So, their story slipped between their fingers.

Don't worry about her. She will be okay.

One day she will only speak of the wonderful moments that filled her with hope.

But if she's honest with herself a year later, she can now admit that she sometimes misses him on cold winter days. She misses the idea of them overcoming every obstacle.

It's on these days she has to forgive herself

for making a difficult decision for the both of
them. She now realizes that she must forgive
herself before she will be able to move forward
one step at a time.
She is patient with herself. She is comfortable
with her pace in life. She gives herself the
grace that she deserves. She is doing her best,
even if her best looks different every day. She
patiently waits to forgive all of the aspects
of their relationship in which she wasn't the
best version of herself. She forgives herself for
not knowing he carried the weight of them
on his shoulders. She forgives herself for not
recognizing their downward spiral before they
collapsed. She forgives herself for not catching
them and trusting that they would last forever.
She forgives herself for that and so much
more. She knows that forgiving oneself is a
process. A process that has no specific outline
or timelines.
She does this so she can put one foot in front of
the other to discover the unknown path that is
ahead.
After all, nothing lasts forever. That phrase
feels so heavy since they walked out of each
other's lives.
There is a coldness within her that seeks

warmth. For now, she wraps herself with the warmth of creating new memories of her own. She will wait for the day she can be this new version of herself that is slowly emerging from the cocoon of grief.

Despite the pain she is learning how to face her fears, wipe her own tears, and fall in love with life again. She is learning to love life on her own terms because she believes in herself wholeheartedly. She trusts in her ability to shift her habits and change her life on her own.

i couldn't see beyond these walls
i imagined a life with you in it all

i couldn't feel us losing grip of a love we once
had
i imagined the rest of my days never feeling
sad

i couldn't hear you through my walls of
loneliness
i imagined the joyful chaos of laughter and
bliss

i couldn't taste the bitterness that was settling
throughout
i imagined the flavors of trips with no chosen
route

i couldn't smell the rain during our storms
i imagined us in all shapes and forms

i couldn't see beyond these walls
yet, here we are watching them fall

beyond a point of no return
my heartache is forever yours

Lisa Annabel

sometimes on lonely nights

the only thing for which i yearn

is a moment with you to discuss
what was learned

(blinded)

what do i know about ghosts?

i can feel them when they're around.
they can't hurt me, but sometimes remind me
of the pain i carry inside.
lost souls in need of guidance.

on occasion i get a visit
she sits with me.
she allows me to feel the emotions that follow
shortly after her visit.
this ghost can only be felt by me and me alone.

on the evenings when the weight of decisions
are heavy on my mind.

oddly, she comes in different forms.

tonight's visit came in the form of a letter to the
one i once loved.
she left me the cruel memory of the time i
apologized for my emotions and i asked for
respect.

it was then i realized that the love i thought we
had was lost years ago.

she reminded me that i deserved more than he
could ever know to give.

after her visits i gently guide her back to the
past where she belongs.
the past that i will only use to grow.

(ghosts)

will i recover?
this is the side
i didn't know i would discover.

this is the other side.
i was cornered to know.

in the beginning,
do we already know
the ending?

(a world without you)

"And the day came when the risk to remain tight in a bud was more painful than the risk it took to blossom."
— Anais Nin

She didn't think she would see this day, ever.
She gladly gave up the days of being single for a life with him.
To create life with him.
However, here she is sometime later.
Single and changed.
Renewed.
Some days she feels painfully strong. Other days, she radiates light and positivity.
She was forced to heal the heartache that was left behind from a marriage that didn't celebrate a ten-year anniversary.
Maybe she got too comfortable. Maybe she allowed herself to get lost in the ideal couple she desperately wanted them to become, but never did.
She knows that there are days he probably hurts too.
She no longer carries the guilt of the most challenging decisions of her life.
She always told him that she could never live without him.
She was right.

The girl he knew died when she accepted that
they weren't meant to continue this journey
together.
She died multiple times, and she had to make
all the funeral arrangements to lay to rest the
naïve version of herself.
She put on her wedding dress one last time
on what would have been their ten-year
anniversary. She saw herself one last time,
so she could let go of what could've been,
should've been, and never became.
Every now and then she whispers to herself
that a year ago she wanted him to save her
from making the decision to walk away. In
their time together she could never articulate
what she needed from him. She couldn't
because she no longer had the energy to tell
him what to do to save her. She no longer
wanted to tell him how to love her.
She can bravely say that her voice doesn't
shake anymore when she speaks of what
happened, and that sometimes scares her.
It's as if with every retell of the ending, she
grew stronger.
With every tear she quietly shed, she watered
the beautiful blooms within her.
The blooms that are flourishing into the

woman she is becoming through her disappointment. The woman she proudly shows the world.

One that is wiser, stronger, and unapologetic for all the beautiful imperfections within her soul.

She has painfully learned that instead of giving her backstory, she would rather let others know who she is today.

Her backstory has its place, and it is in the past. The past that cannot be changed, shifted, or altered.

It stays forever in place. She chooses to leave it there and discover the new version of herself that is willing to do whatever it takes to love and respect herself again.

tonight i went back in time
to talk about you and me
we held each other close
like the future didn't exist

i went back
to tell you how much i loved you

suddenly i realize
this is only a dream

i can't describe
the pain i carry quietly inside

(time machine)

what if…
i don't want any more heartache?
i want to sing and dance this life alone.

what if…
i don't know how to love with limits and
boundaries
because i only picture my future with you?

what if…
in my journey to find me
i decide that being alone is easier?

what if…
i want to see the world only through my eyes?
slowly, becoming my own best friend
so that i am the only one to blame
for life's inevitable disappointments.

what if…
i told you that i only know how to live for
others?
i am scared to open myself to another because i
have failed too many times before.

what if...
i know that i am the only one that stands between
me, myself, and i
among all that requires love?

(overthinking heart)

and suddenly i turn the page
realizing that the chapter
has come to an end

learning from my reflection
while soaking in the lesson

i am left with a clue…

the next chapter
no longer includes you

(ending story)

"When you fight yourself to discover the real you,
there is only one winner."
—Stephen Richards

Time. It's the one thing we find so difficult to manage. We ask for more of it, yet we waste it when it's gifted. Time is so precious. Time is what the pandemic gave us all. Just enough time to take a long, hard look at our lives. For some, that pause in time changed our lives forever and amplified all that was fractured within us. We are now left to either address those fears that stare at us blatantly in the face or we can choose to hide them and allow them to slowly continue to consume our peace.

I sat with the time given and realized how much of it I had spent unaware of what was happening within me. In a world that is so busy trying to stay busy, I stood there as I watched life spin around me. The innocent version of myself became a faint image in the mirror, and the woman who was emerging was unknown to me.

The woman who stares back shares her wounds with me and asks for them to be healed. Wounds that can only be healed with what I decide to do with my time.

What we often fail to realize is that we are all given time, and it is what we do with time that matters.

Therefore, I will take time to meet this version of myself.
I will take time to piece me back together and build a home within me.
I will take time to heal my heart.
I will take time to mourn my past life as many times as I need to, guilt free.
I will take time to pause and breathe.
I will take time to feel all the pain within me.
I will take time to set myself free from the many shadows that won't let me be.

I have too many goals to live in the panic room in my mind. A panic room that was created by life's many disenchantments. It is difficult to describe what happens within me unexpectedly. I want to be heard, but I can't find the words. My insecurities begin to whisper all that is wrong with me.

Every piece of faith is shaken.
I want to breathe, but I can't.
I want to listen, but I can't.
I want to break free, but I can't.
I drown in the silence that falls over me.
I want to give up.
I just want to loosen the knot that suffocates
the real me.

However, I know that the only person who can
save me from here is the stronger version of me.

The woman I am making time to meet.
I want to become the winner of this fight that is
only me against me, so that I don't waste any
more time in this panic room known to others
as anxiety.

i'm tired of me...

anxiety

depression

all the turbulence within
won't let me be.

(internal chaos)

my past calls every now & then
ignoring the call
my mind opens a door
i tiptoe in

our story is written on the walls
my eyes fill with tears
i stop to breathe
slowly stepping out

i remember the lonely nights
hold myself
knowing these emotions will take time

my overthinking
losing sleep
remind me of the reasons to leave

i close the door behind me
wishing you the best
without regret

i hope you're happy without me

(don't pick up)

a mess was left
to be cleaned, even if my heart's bereft

there was no plea
pain felt within me

filled with regret, loneliness, and hurt
this pain i feel must convert

give me time
so that piece by piece
i find my peace

(our mess)

are you over the heartache?
a heartache comes with lessons
lessons not for *them*
lessons for *me*

short answer
no.

the pain remains
but not the same
and not for *them*
but for *me*

pain that leads the way
to find a home
a home
to me

(love & learn)

Home.

This is a place where she can live and feel her
most authentic self.
If this is the definition of home,
then she has made her home in so many people
she loved,
deeply.

(misplaced love)

And I Felt It All

slowly,
i began to shift and change

strange,
because i lost my way

not knowing if i should stay
i searched among the gray

and there among the trees
a glimmer of light
and a guiding breeze

led me to the home
that is now within me

(home)

Lisa Annabel

flow
to
grow

(slow down)

And I Felt It All

and there I sat,
still for a moment in time,
listening to the gentle whispers of the crashing
waves rolling by…
reminding me
what it is to be free.

stillness isn't what we do;
it's what we feel deep within.
it's how we renew.

and there I sat,
still for a moment in time,
waiting for the feeling of peace to remind me
of the beauty of being alive.

(coastlines)

Lisa Annabel

i was given a gift
a gift filled with darkness
a reflection of my patterns
a reflection of my shadows
my unhealed wounds.

mine.

a once-in-a-lifetime gift.
i learned to value it.
i learned to grow from it.
i learned to experience it in its entirety.

a gift i used to deconstruct myself
so i could build a healed version just for me.

(thank you)

how will i know i have found thee?
when they are gentle with my soul,
that will be the goal.
i question, is that the key?
perfection isn't expected
and trauma is not projected.
as i sit and stare at the sea,
how committed am i
to understand why?
if searching for a mate,
i foresee emotional maturity
someone to offer security.
i am learning that this responsibility is in my
fate.
it's me who i must create.

(the mate i create for me)

let it flow
flow + put yourself on center stage
center stage to live
live *fully*

so you can discover
your *beauty* among the mess
your *magic* between the chaos
your *extraordinary* when you're overwhelmed

let it flow
flow + find gratitude
gratitude for the joy and love you have to give

when you let it flow
you grow

(flow)

too fit
too big
too tall
too loud
too much
too small
too smart
too strong

too obvious
that i am
too loved
to worry
how the world sees me

(enough)

a soul like mine

would it feel what i feel
would it know my secrets
would it speak words that heal

a soul like mine

could it cure me of my mess
could it understand my depth
could it empathize when i'm in distress
could it comfort me so i can catch my breath

a soul like mine

should it sing its truths
should it adapt to life's design
should it stand with strong roots
should it give compassion & align
should it dance to the rhythm of the flutes

to love a soul like mine

(…)

she is
i know
the only home i longed for
she is
i know
the only reason i want to grow
she is
i know
the only life i can't let go
she is
i know
the only fire within my soul
she is
the only love
i know

(forever she)

like the sunrise over a clear blue ocean
like a calm breeze bringing in a crashing wave

she is beauty

like the peony in full bloom
like the gentle touch of a petal against your
skin

she is soft

she was and still is all that radiates love

even when
you didn't see her

(bella)

who am i in my solitude?

quiet…with my thoughts that haunt
calm…when i forget my past
soft, yet strong…
because in my solitude
no one sees
the brokenness
that hides within
and reminds me
that the love i feel
will lift me again
and again

(free to be me)

"Two things you will never have to chase: true friends & true love."
—Mandy Hale

Opening up is a risk.
A risk of being misunderstood.
A risk of being seen as you are and being swept off your feet.
A risk of being rejected or even worse,
not given an opportunity to see where the relationship could have continued to bloom.
However, the narrative has changed because she now knows when to let people go. She will no longer allow relationships to fade into the dark. She faces the difficult moment head-on and expresses her emotions. She knows how to gracefully pack up her emotions and continue her path. She may have tears in her eyes. She is not only okay with it, but unapologetic for expressing her emotions. Holding back her tears is no longer an option.
She liked him. She connected with him like she hadn't with another person before.
There were so many things she wanted to explore with him. She didn't think a half-hearted connection was one of them.
So, it's with a knot in her chest that she

says goodbye. Her heart recognizes kind
and soft connections. Along with those rare
connections, she seeks peace in a meaningful
relationship.
She will no longer stand by for the moment
when he tells her that another woman has
caught his eye. When we truly care about a
person, those experiences are categorized as
heartaches.

Maybe she shouldn't have shared so much
about her past.
Maybe there were things he silently tested her
on and she failed.
Or maybe the connection for him was less than
his willingness to explore something good.
Something soft.
Something genuine.

Or maybe he was just a person to show her
that she now has the bravery to close doors
and no longer wait around for others to value
all that she brings into their lives.

She knows that she isn't stuck and will no
longer accept patterns of behavior that don't
serve her and only bring harm.

So, she throws in the towel and walks away
knowing that one day the right person will
know the diamond of a woman they have
in front of them. They will give themselves
without reservation.

She doesn't chase; instead she waits. Waits
for the person who wants her as much as she
wants them.
dear love,
i know we haven't met,
but i want to express how much it's meant
to live this life with you.
every struggle has been worth it
and in the turbulence we find another version
of ourselves.
in those moments
i want to show you how much more my love
for you grows
that our love for one another is
gentle
authentic
and real.
if only fairy tales can truly show the ordinary
that is extraordinary
then will we value true love
love that is built

not found
love that is
you
and me.

(letter for the future)

Lisa Annabel

but with you

every day will be
a gentle touch
a calming conversation
a reflection of all the joy i have in me

the chemistry
i didn't know i need

(future love)

love,
if it's temporary
i don't want you near
just leave me
for letting go is what i fear

(passing by)

and
my coffee
began to
taste more
delightful

i met you.

(taste again)

the only *me*
in the mirror with no lies
i am unbeautiful
inside and out
and it's impossible that
he sees *me*

(bottom up)

Lisa Annabel

i like you
give me one night just for me

i saw you from afar
eyes meet

give me a minute
let's just see

to watch you
is to know how to breathe

i like you
give me one night just for me

(and so we meet)

teach me.

how do i console you
when your heart is bruised?
what do you need from me
when you are drained?
tell me,
how do i add to your joy?

teach me.

how do i help you
when you've gone astray?
what gentleness do i use
when you feel confused?
tell me,
how do i become your lover and your friend?

teach me,
for i do not know
the inner workings of your mind.

all i know is mine.

(learn you)

Lisa Annabel

let me
show you
all that's new

let's go to the moon
let's find a different view

that's just for me and you

hold my hand
i don't know the way
together we can get away

don't stay
i promise
the gray will go away

(the moon)

i want you
and together make
love

because to crave you

is to be
      admired
      desired
      seen
i want you
and together create
intimacy

(love is intimacy)

my admiration?

our talks
about nothing and everything all at once,
our laughs
about our mistakes and imperfectly timed
puns,
our fingers intertwined
that give comfort among a storm,
our hallmark of clarity and calmness
when we speak to one another's heart,
our easy walks through disagreements
without a need to determine who is right,
our intimacy
that is built beyond our silk sheets,
our transparency of trust
that we consciously build and protect.

my admiration
is you and me
teaching me that loving can be this free.

(building together)

negotiating imperfection every day
that is our love

raw and rare

negotiating whether to agree or disagree
gracefully incompatible
you are sometimes a mystery to me

imperfections boldly seen
appreciating what we bring
i will go nowhere
but rather work on being a pair

you and i are human
between us perfection can't exist
so we will learn to love
without regret
as long as there is respect

(not a perfect love)

Dedication

To the person who forever changed me. Because of you I had to reach deep within myself to become the woman I am today.
This version of myself thanks you for every moment we shared, both the beautiful and the heartaches.
Thank you for loving me the best way you knew how to love, even if it wasn't forever.

To my readers, may my prose and poems help you feel less alone. I want you to know that you can use your pain to heal and grow.

All you have felt will serve a purpose. Maybe it wasn't how you wanted to experience love, but just know that your heartache can prepare you for something that is genuine and right for you. It will all make sense once you embrace your storm and enjoy the seeds of healing you have planted.

And finally, to those who knew how to love me through my darkness, I will forever be grateful for the compassion you showed me and the love you gave me.
Thank you.

Printed in the USA
CPSIA information can be obtained
at www.ICGtesting.com
LVHW041206280723
753392LV00009B/1032